The Loneliness Jacket

Charles Hansmann

The Loneliness Jacket

Charles Hansmann

Apprentice House
Baltimore, Maryland

Printed in the United States of America
First Edition

ISBN: 978-1-934074-61-9

Published by Apprentice House
The Future of Publishing…Today!

Apprentice House
Communication Department
Loyola University Maryland
4501 N. Charles Street
Baltimore, MD 21210
410.617.5265
www.ApprenticeHouse.com

Versions of these poems appeared in the following magazines:

bottle rockets: "Incipit"

Chrysanthemum (Austria): "Cocoon," "Doldrums Entry"

Contemporary Haibun: "Apprentice"

Contemporary Haibun Online: "The Recycling Center"

Frogpond: "Birthday Hike," "En Pointe," "Likeness," "Slant," "Vivien"

Ink, Sweat & Tears (England): "Homeland," "Seduction of the Poem"

Kokako (New Zealand): "Scrub Highway"

The Lilliput Review: "bird nest, and threads"

LYNX: "Came First," "Noon"

Modern Haibun & Tanka Prose: "Jesus Saves," "Paparazzi"

Modern Haiku: "Layer"

The Prose Poem Project: "Cottage"

Snap Poetry Review: "The Loneliness Jacket," "Sonoran Winter"

Stylus (Australia): "In Plain Sight," "Missing Me One Place"

Wild Goose Poetry Review: "Catch and Release," "Renunciation," "Sun Fish"

And in the following anthologies:

Touching: Poems of Love, Longing, and Desire (Fearless Books, 2010): "Likeness"

The Light in Ordinary Things (Fearless Books, 2009): "The Recycling Center"

Dover Beach and My Back Yard (British Haiku Society, 2007): "At Sea" and "In Step"

for Eileen

what I hoped it would be

c o n t e n t s

Charles Hansmann grew up in the dairy-farming country of east-central Wisconsin. He has worked as a gandy dancer in his home state, a refrigerated-truck driver in Florida, an industrial photographer in California, a warehouse man in Hawaii, a waiter in Arizona, and a lawyer in New York. He holds degrees in English, philosophy, and law; and lives in Sea Cliff, New York, with his wife, Eileen Kennedy.

Missing Me One Place

I turn my face to the sun but can't get enough,
walk across town and stare up the Hudson
to the sharp line of trees on the opposite bluff.

Failing to fetch me at first keep encouraged.

In Riverside Park I watch high-tech kites with multiple control lines
harry the pigeons, a willow snatch leaves
from the long-sleeved grass. I'm carrying Whitman's

Song of Myself, a pocket edition, covet the bench and the collar-up bask.
A boy pounds his mitt while his friend zips his jacket,
tosses me the ball and it stings when I catch it.

Missing me one place search another.

Stray footprint in mulch,
a crocus poking up through the arch —
some lines I know by heart as soon as I read them.

Apprentice

Now! my sister calls, and conjured snowflakes fall
through summer heat. She has worked for weeks

cutting them out of her notebook,
her scissors persistent beyond boredom,
and from that window above me
overturned her basket. The thin paper flakes

so lazy in their fall I can see up through them
her tiny white teeth bright with permission
she cannot grant. *Jump up here!*
she shouts down, as if now,

touched by her worked miracle,
magic will come easy to me.

> *bird nest! and threads*
> *from my red sweater*
> *I find there*

The Recycling Center

He walks slowly as we leave behind
the house now empty of all
but his needs, his stories
important again, his youth and early setting up
by which I once learned the workings of a world
that reported all its wonders.

We follow a soft lane, skirt the marsh behind the plant
where discarded paper is trucked and processed.
He's tolerant
of the fly-away dailies that litter our path,
points out from time to time
some sign that nature takes this in stride —

> *a turtle poking*
> *its nose into*
> *an old edition*

Cottage

The blanket we hunker
under is heavy. We're pressed

so deep the spread covers us flat, and the bed
looks made while we are still in it.

Our room is the same without us, loose
shadowy sleeves through closet louvers,

faint radio static untuning the station.
Disappearing like this we don't exist

but still go on thinking,
or so we are thinking.

> *rainy-day door, your*
> *shoulder nudging it*
> *begrudgingly open*

Renunciation

Gulls crying out on
updrafts sail
flying over dunes, now
trot the air like
town dogs, now blow
bunched like litter.

Bluesy on guitar you
couldn't play up tempo,
but you could make
your fingers hurt, on those strings,
and every note you'd make
me hear it.

> *breathtakingly sparse*
> *new leaves at dawn*
> *claiming our view*

The Loneliness Jacket

You wear it and it snows: tracks
empty the park outside the museum.

A promo pen blues
your breast-pocket lining, and a snag starts to pull

at your sleeve. *Last one left
is as good as extinction.* So says the quote

on the leaking plastic. But someone's pinkie
shined of wax on this second-hand tweed

flecks the lapel with an old, cleared hearing –
conversation, recorded in a stain.

You button up and listen in.
 for this snow is like talk in the sign-language trees,

a thing you name, and the name sticks,
windows lighting up in the dinosaur wing.

Catch and Release

In a factory where nothing is done without asking,
in air so heavy metal
filings can float on it, we punch out
at midnight for the three-week layoff.
We drive through the night and then through

Minnesota, which except that we don't live there
is just like Wisconsin.
Then South Dakota, the grass so little nurtured
it seems we wear paths just by pointing at
the places we would walk to.

One long ride with tent and fly rods till we camp in Montana.
It comes down to what we're doing this for:
him to forget the girl who wanted
nothing of his dreams, who had, I thought,
a need I knew, so me to forget her too.

Sonoran Winter

Lizards huffing igneous
in the plaster? We listen

by the sockets and the light switch,
certain that adobe reverts back to mud

and makes short work of retro-fitted wiring.
But every desert drip

echoes *failed* disaster: the overhead holds steady.
We chide ourselves with laughter and step outside

admiring stucco sky. The folding chair —
not worth bringing in: our buttocks sagged

its canvas sling — perks rain
through clogged pinnate leaves, the pepper tree's,

and some from our lemon verbena,
a nearly imperceptible stain

ponding xylophonic
on the patio of fauna flags,

indigenous, inlaid, our favorite porcelain
tink of the javelina.

In Plain Sight

There's a bear rug draped over our footboard,
and on mornings like this the bed seems to hold us in a hug.

The hide's a hundred years old but still in good shape,
bought in Leadville, Colorado,

on a car-camping trip the year we eloped.
We lugged it east like a catch and spread it out in the den,

overlapping the edge of the thinning Persian.
Even in socks we never stepped on the fur,

always walked around it, though once, not looking,
you stumbled on the head, and for pity's sake

moved it to the footboard, dark glass a dead
ringer for the eyes.

Likeness

She is so like me that when we quarrel
it seems we're laying claim to what

we'd disappear without.
And when we thump

the back seat like a bed I keep losing
through my mind just who is doing

what. Boundaries
erode. There goes

the territorial stalking,
and there the pool that used to show

my face. Here comes the woman looking
out through my reflection.

En Pointe

Someone's daughter
loves to dance.

Any unheard
music seems to do,

and any partner.
The table's shimmed leg

attends her lifted heel.
She gains a peek

beyond the windowsill.

> *ballet slippers*
> *pigeon-toed*
> *beside the bed*

At Sea

We're anchored in the shallow part of the bay,
between the riprap and the rock shore,

showing brown algae on our hull
and hammered by rain that should have held off till late fall.

Every morning there's a clatter of clam shells
on the deck, gulls

swooping down to their breakfast.
They're defiant, but wary,

and when they are challenged they spread their skank wings
and flap like stiff laundry to the sky.

We finally set out, big wind all night, no sleep.
Outside our sail the draft behind wind

pulls us into its own receding. We're drawn
toward fright, but it's worth it for this:

We see the maxim – darkest, then dawn.

Incipit

I am born in a leap
year and beat the added day by one.
At twelve I count
forward three months to fix my date
of conception. A new solitude
stirs, the union of two
warm gametes. My coming together occurs

at the end of May, my father blue-
penciling theses, my mother moth-
balling her woolens, her lightweight cottons
cradled in armfuls down from the attic.
Then some pretty picnic
dress tossed on on impulse, hair undone
in whispers to me impossibly known.

> *sandals by the swing*
> *in sun in shade in sun in shade*
> *bare feet pumping*

Cocoon

This caterpillar's hibernaculum

is flawed, frost
invaded. No butterfly or moth

bums

an insulated ride. The metal playground slide
conducts the chill the children (summertime)

find so thrilling, in winter sled the hill —

your woolen mitten
frozen to the ladder rail.

Jesus Saves

Trowel-full of dirt on the polished lid –
it sounds like a cat jumping down off a porch rail,
the brindled cat that slipped through the screen door
at the desert roadside grocery we once stopped at for sodas,
and bought candy bars too, Payday, since nuts wouldn't melt
and would replenish lost salt.
We'd had a long drive and were feeling road-giddy.
They tossed their wrappers to the back and I batted them down,
goaltender of the window.
Good save! my father shouted, his words
woofered in the wind, and my mother shouted back
the words on a billboard.

Homeland

You dream I am dead and you visit me in heaven. It's a place
we can't sink, water so salty we float without treading.
We cannot drown there even if we want to. There's no place else
for the sodden soul to go.
Even in heaven the sky flashes at night, and we find our berth
in an open-air greenhouse. The flowers fold up
and it's time for you to leave. Your boss back on earth
says you're going to be canned if you're ever late again.

When you tell me this dream still wet from your shower
I wish the morning had a shoulder I could hug beyond our own,
a towel to guide the day with a vigorous rubdown.
I am the person you fear will die,
and daily I earn my desire to be here.
It takes a sweeping out, a place to keep clean, no hijinks of the road.
Nothing deserves our mortal fear less than camping out by the wayside.
That's not the land of appointments, and I've got one tomorrow

for an MRI. I go crazy in that cylinder, like live ammunition.
But your dream boss relents and lets you come with me.
I expand the tight chamber with a vision of the sea
in the translated novel you pull from your purse. I blink back at the curve
I can fog with my breath, and I'm aware as the tube sucks me into its core
of all of the ways I will never get out. Yet I'll take the scant comfort:
If while I am in there the suitcase plutonium levels our city,
I'll be close to the page you are reading when it happens.

> *we hear it again*
> *at work on the roof patch*
> *trying to get in*

Sun Fish

Rings in sand
the fish limned spawning
cast glimmers out of the pond
and into the morning's
bailing can,
rimmed with rust
and
floating at your feet.
A dragonfly depletes
the lily frond
and alights
its iridescent rainbow
on your cane pole.
It's August,
your bobber's tugged
toward mud.
You've got a bite.

Seduction of the Poem

I am talking you away from the lover
who promised to be faithful. That isn't a typo
and that lover's still me.
Get into the car. That's all that it takes.
You're being talked to the place where nothing you choose
determines what happens.
For haven't you wanted to ride in the rain
with the top down ever since watching the wind
blow the spume off those waves at the Cliff House?
I tell you we are going to go fast.
That way the windshield's a vertical umbrella,
and your thin cotton shirt will not start to reveal you.
I don't have to know. It's your adventure, not mine,
and right now you don't care what is under your clothes.
Right now you are watching the streak of these wipers
for that dry explication that lies between lines.
And this corner we are turning,
this corner that's maybe no more than a bend,
puts behind you any notion that anyone who knows you
still has you under tabs.
For now you are my sweetheart.
In this grip our world's glove
turns the wheel that will steer us.
In this fist our palms lie palm to palm.

Doldrums Entry

Sand isn't land, nor is it
sea. Shore
is where both or neither
want to be.
Can't say the same about air.
This boat won't stir
until it freshens. In the meantime,
calm invents inverted lessons:
to do there is nothing, hence this jotting.
And who's to say the sky
doesn't need every inch beyond the earth
to make it blue?
Blue because for all
purposes endless, nothing gets past.
Though now there's a breeze,
and wind amends this
stall — fast.

Layer

Butchering chickens it's my job to fend off
the geeks,
keep them from eating the severed heads.
Cats, of course,
but I'm thinking geeks, those carny grotesques
of the whistling windpipe.

There is chop and spurt and flurry, a bifurcated
frenzy, then lull.
This one, head-free,
flaps from the hatchet block to a nest she makes
calmly in the grass,
near the garden —

and while the hooding eyes in the heads that I'm
protecting
watch from the pile where they've fallen,
lays her last, perfect egg,
though the shell,
still soft, won't harden.

Came First

The chickens bock bock bocking in
the early morning coop, the heat of the egg in

my hand, I think

hens sit on nests these cold dawn hours to
keep their bottoms warm.

Scrub Highway

The road is an arrow, though our map
shows it squiggly. I'm glad we've got that

straightened out. Scant rain last week,
and now the desert flora, its spectrum narrow,

squanders the drought. We've had
this map for years. It shows

us places no one knows
to go. We like to say

it got us here. Got us here
but still unwieldy. Folded wrong way, the crease

doubled back, our map winds wayless down
a shortcut of ruts. For the road

is a trickster: it is crossed
by coyote: the numbers are fixed

on the mileage signs, and somewhere ahead
the places are wary.

> *cantina courtyard*
> *in the lull between plates*
> *a placemat fading*

Slant

Some times of day don't show themselves direct.
They're just reflected on

the surface, skittish

moments slinking down to drink, rippling
indistinct the instant

that we see them. Then turn around.

Some times of day only follow on
their memory, haven't happened till

they're past, a set sun

lighting up the hill behind,
reappearing as we climb.

>   *up all night*
>   *to see what cats see*
>   *alley moon*

Paparazzi

I put milk in my coffee and step outside,
the morning photographic in its clarity,
detail of each twig printed on the trees,
and a twist of birch against a dark grove
drawn forward from the background with
highlighted focus.

It's a cheat to see it like this,

like that photo my father
was so thrilled to have taken.
He had it enlarged and framed in green matte
and tacked it inside the door of his closet.
A celebrity shot, he said to me once,
I got that tree's *autograph*.

Noon

Time again, each morning when we wake,
and place too —
us, then me, you — separate
sides for swinging out our legs,
a day taking place, we say
(though meaning taking time),
as approach succeeded by withdrawal,
as if the highlight were exactly that,
our lives meridian-centric, a countdown
to an apex moment,
the church bell, the firehouse whistle,
and then a count away from it.

> *in the clock-tower shade*
> *lunchers eyeing their watches*

Vivien

The V between
her fingers — there are shouts
from the rue de la Harpe.

Vive! flies up
to our third-floor window.
Long live my marrow

pressed in this wedge,
Vive! every part of me
tightened in this vise —

> *raised wings, a sparrow*
> *landing on the ledge*

Boulevardiers

We drink cappuccino
at a sidewalk café.
She has smuggled us a bag
of almond biscotti,
passes me a piece
with a great show of stealth
beneath the glass-top table —
louche afternoon,
the cadging sparrows
pulling on cig butts.

The John Translations

I pass a marquee in Mexico City.
Now playing is *Vasolino*.
I recognize the poster: John
Travolta and Olivia
Newton John. Pigeons crumb
the sidewalk, a bum pan-
handling bread. The moment un-
folds to my vagabond
summer in Paris, so long
ago all the girls
are eighteen, the books
only French: *Rue de la Sardine*
by John Steinbeck.

Birthday Hike

My bottle filled with mountain runoff
chills me suddenly new
to old skin. The uphill ache sets in.

Snow fell the winter
I thrilled to be twenty.
Its melt I ford these decades later.

Time for a breather —
scuffed boots
on polished stones.

The rest makes me cold. I set
stones in a ring and spill through these woods
for their bounty of kindling.

Where else to warm my heart but at
the campfire story it's my turn to tell —
silhouette in the hemlock all ears.

In Step

I'm finding age in my bones as if turning to stone

were a way to fix my form
when my cells no longer can.
Or the hollow I will leave as clay
hardens an outline of my decay.

Whether I'm to be petrified or fossilized

the sky keeps coming to the window
and the errant birds keep thudding against
this darkness. Who has a better sense

of how the light is changing
than those who read not by

the light, but only the light. This light

today touches your face and impresses
me with this memory.
When the mark it has made lifts out,
who knows toward what passage

or glass those wings will fly. I
stand here hobbled while
the thought goes running by.

> *upturned beetle*
> *someone's footprint*
> *filled with rain*

The future of publishing...today!

Apprentice House is the country's only campus-based, student-staffed book publishing company. Directed by professors and industry professionals, it is a nonprofit activity of the Communication Department at Loyola University in Maryland.

Using state-of-the-art technology and an experiential learning model of education, Apprentice House publishes books in untraditional ways. This dual responsibility as publishers and educators creates an unprecedented collaborative environment among faculty and students, while teaching tomorrow's editors, designers, and marketers.

Outside of class, progress on book projects is carried forth by the AH Book Publishing Club, a co-curricular campus organization supported by Loyola University's Office of Student Activities.

Student Project Team for *The Loneliness Jacket:*
    Godfrey Von Nordeck '12

Eclectic and provocative, Apprentice House titles intend to entertain as well as spark dialogue on a variety of topics. Financial contributions to sustain the press's work are welcomed. Contributions are tax deductible to the fullest extent allowed by the IRS.

To learn more about Apprentice House books or to obtain submission guidelines, please visit www.ApprenticeHouse.com.

Apprentice House
Communication Department
Loyola University in Maryland
4501 N. Charles Street
Baltimore, MD 21210
Ph: 410-617-5265 • Fax: 410-617-2198
info@apprenticehouse.com